PROSPECTS

PROSPECTS

JUDITH HALL

LOUISIANA STATE UNIVERSITY PRESS

BATON ROUGE

Published by Louisiana State University Press
www.lsupress.org

LSU Press Paperback Original

DESIGNER: Barbara Neely Bourgoyne
TYPEFACE: Garamond

Cover image: Jim Dine, *Hose Lamp,* 1968, Indianapolis Museum of Art at Newfields, Delavan
Smith Fund, 69.62.4 © 2020 Jim Dine/Artists Rights Society (ARS), New York.

Library of Congress Cataloging-in-Publication Data
Names: Hall, Judith, 1951– author.
Title: Prospects / Judith Hall.
Description: Baton Rouge : Louisiana State University Press, [2020] | "LSU Press Paperback
    Original"—Title page verso.
Identifiers: LCCN 2020005900 (print) | LCCN 2020005901 (ebook) | ISBN 978-0-8071-
    7263-6 (paperback) | ISBN 978-0-8071-7422-7 (pdf) | ISBN 978-0-8071-7423-4 (epub)
Subjects: LCGFT: Poetry.
Classification: LCC PS3558.A3695 P766 2020 (print) | LCC PS3558.A3695 (ebook) | DDC
    811/.54—dc23
LC record available at https://lccn.loc.gov/2020005900
LC ebook record available at https://lccn.loc.gov/2020005901

I SAW A MAN PURSUING THE HORIZON ;
ROUND AND ROUND THEY SPED.
I WAS DISTURBED AT THIS ;
I ACCOSTED THE MAN.
"IT IS FUTILE," I SAID,
"YOU CAN NEVER"—

"YOU LIE," HE CRIED,
AND RAN ON.

—STEPHEN CRANE

CONTENTS

PROSPECTS

THE BOY'S GRACE; OR, PESSIMISM

After Peter, Huck, Marcel

Between one adventure and another
I felt so lonesome I
Used to go to bed

On the wind's back and
Stooping down so as the
Candle was no longer burning

I remember about my mother.
Throw in the fancy touches.
"Kiss me just once more."

And I know not why
It don't work for me
Having her there at all.

The upper world had called
Gliding swift along, dead silent,
Not to disturb the moonlight.

You asked me to list qualifications, fit, my "fit," but couldn't I have told you yesterday when we met? Plus I am, as you said, ready, willing, able to work. What work you have, said you have, I don't know. "Ask away, ambitious chap," you said, I mean I heard. "Chap" a funny word my mother favored. "Chap." Willing to work evenings I was told to say. Weekends. Whole ball of wax. Proves sticking power. What is sticking if not willing? The best stick around your building, knock, I remember which knock enters. Your joke about a pair o' knockers. Remember I am the one who laughed. Sincerely,

Needed, but not wanted, not really.
Gave the application too much feeling.

Surprise
Surprise

Everyone in line ahead of me
Will praise him. Sincerely, sincerely

Today
Wanted today.

Praise drifts back to me as if for laughs.
Don't mention it. Thanks.

WITH INGENIOUS HALF-SQUAT THRUSTS
ROUND THE TREES AND

HEAVILY FORTIFIED HORIZON—

NEVER DOUBTING
EFFORT ALONE "THE MIRACLE

ESCAPE FROM MARTYRDOM"—NEVER
DOUBTING, DOUBLING EFFORT—NOISY,

NOT TO MENTION—MOIST—ISN'T IT?

Situation normal: all fingers up
In well-known locality.

No ease from apprehension.

Every man for himself.

Damn little to offer any business
Larger than a hotdog stand.

"I could sell 20 per week, yes *SUH!*"

"Slap some chili on it, pal."

No mayo. No banan-o.
Hold gripes to a minimum.

No relish whatever. Want onion?

All out of liquor and liquor

By any other name: morale,
Incentive. Sweet incentive.

VISIBLE, TINIER PURSUIT.

ROUND AND ROUND, I

SAW IT FLICKER,
GLEAM—HAPPINESS
SHOULD. HOWEVER FLEETING SUBMISSIONS
TO CERTAINTY.

AND GOOD TO KNOW

I SUPPOSE. "AFTER THE FACT." DOUBTLESS.

These, his last,
     employers, dead
Inexplicably and
Unavailable
  to praise his diligence,

Cast a shadow on his prospects, and he sighed.
Before all this, he
Would have lit a pipe and
     mused on the past
In aromatic mauve tobacco . . . Shadows
Baffled pleasantly
  the better rug

Once a bear.
    Grizzly bear.
He would have enjoyed a smoke with a bear.
Hibernation is
  not unlike a job you fail to love.

He would have enjoyed
Some banter on, and amiable disputation of,
His claim. Or
    on job loss, in general;
On night air, the fanfare above a curve, a star,
If suitably
  asparkle in public.

A SENTENCE showing no sign of ending for why

Follow what by all rights will end

Horribly probably

As if making in the middle of a prison break a cry

FOR WHOM FOR WHAT causes

A sound that will

Never be a better protective bravura than silence

When it ends with a pillowcase

The cry unless

Appeals come to think of it persuade with a cry

Commute a sentence to cries

Left on a tangled

Unexamined island among clams flung amulets

A story in a rehabilitated storm

Cooperates rolling over

Pleasant isn't it in a buckled bamboo rocker

Flecked with autumn sunlight as

Sincere an amber as

An amateur in court dreaming someone else's whiskey

Leaves a halo on a palm and when touched

Extends to fingers strangers

Good behavior good as small and smaller talk

Tossed back and forth

An equilibrium between an ending and escape.

From the DANAË COLLECTION

Of Danaë, whom Jupiter made pregnant with his fertile gold,
and that though she was imprisoned in a tower.
—OVID

Take this misshapen oval, for example, gold
Coin lion, whose protective menace is a laugh.

Or this one, where the reeded edges prickle, gold,
Bitten, see? Or finger these heroic profiles.

These, even heavier coins, face down, the gold,
Sticky with the faintest sunny rivulets and whorls

Of semen, smell it? Face up? Sad to say old gold
This soft, very damaged. No inscription, no.

More under the bed, we trust. In more clouded gold
Shoveled high against the walls? The gold-bruised door? Coins

*

EVEN ONE FALLING HAS FOLLOWERS . . . SHOWERS FLUNG

AS HAIL HAIL AS GOLD LAUNCH AN AVALANCHE AIMED

AT SLOWLY NATURALIZED . . . ALIENATION

*

Hoarded, for a future solitude, like fool's gold:
"I am" otherwise "worthy of attention"

*

IRRATIONAL EXUBERANCE . . . IRIDESCENT

BUBBLED ASSET-VALUE BOOM COLLAPSING AND

PENETRATING BADLY . . . AM I CAPITALIZED

*

If privately held? Hit with toxic assets, gold
Unreasonably unreal . . . thing of the past am I

*

OTHERWISE TAKEN FOR . . . AS WHEN A GIVEN TOWER

OPENS TO THE PUBLIC PREHISTORIC GOLD

PAINFULLY INVISIBLE WHEN RAW . . . OTHERWISE

*

Ambitious drizzle claiming to be rain. And gold
Joked about mostly. Tourists. Museums manage

Gold-painted souvenirs sold around the square. Gold,
As from a tower, releases automatic force

Displayed by weight, by date, they laugh: at change, at gold,
At lectures on one perfectly preserved ka-ching.

Bonus: Give or take a rape diorama, gold-
Wrapped cold adventures: chocolates promised if it rains.

They love the tower open when it rains. Rush! Gold!
"Move over." "Fuck you" mouthed another from afar.

THE GIRL'S WILL; OR, OPTIMISM

After Alice, Lolita, Candy, Candide, and Alice Again

"Curiouser and curiouser!" cried _____
Half-naked, kneeling, turning about on
"*Darn* Daddy anyway!" she said
Once upon a time.
Something interesting is sure to

Grow large again, for really
The sex interests of children
The heavy breathing of the
Best. For I am infinitely
Growing and growing, and very soon

With a yelp of delight
Stirring in a little girl
Her terrible selfishness, how it
Was an indispensable part of
Thinking I should be free.

"*Please* mind what you're doing!"
"This is a free country."
The girl was quite excited,
The best of all possible
Riddles that have no answers.

Look at it this way:
                    I've been asked to sign a contract
For, say, five years with a weak option on another five.
The job? Must be attractive,

Companionable,
                    patient, unemotional (this
The challenge); and I must be easy and chilly enough
To forgive the ridicule.

Forget about love.
                    I think I can manage the job.
Yes. Flotillas of kisses, forgotten. Hangovers from
Adolescence, nothing else.

The compensation?
                    Deposit whatever I save
Out of a weekly house and personal budget of $3,850.
Also purchased in my name,

Once a week, a $500 bond.
                            I have a clear deed promised to
His too-damn-Italian pleasure palace near Ann Arbor;
20-acre pear orchard.

On the death of Joe,
                    I have all cash-on-hand plus 1/8
Of all stock in a 10-million-dollar business (this held
In escrow for 17 years;

I.e., I acquire
                    earnings only for 17 years;
After that, the stock reverts to me, my heirs.) Not bad,
Founding a family fortune.

Can you see beyond
                    your finer sensibilities
To elementary financial accounts? I will work
To keep Joe alive, work hard

His last years; these, his
                    happiest. Saturday, rain, shine,
He blows in from Winnipeg; we marry. Due time.
If you never understand

What I had to learn,
                    I understand. Pray you never . . .
I am in his house, the yellow one, and you should hear me
On the organ. Easier,

So much easier,
                    than piano. I depend on
Music. Wind under pressure, constant pressure, very real.
The rest is histrionic.

Tried that too that—Gift—To be simply—Adrift—
Drunk—Punk—Puke—
For which the sucker prize—Pregnant—Priceless—
Also tried—

Sold that shit a long while—Cheered me, sure—Superior
The fringe life—
Dangle down to Coral Gables selling oranges—
Any road—

All right—Twisting cheer from messy and familiar
Strands of—Learned
Futility—Adrift—On little left to try—
Cheered me—Sure—

The shine—Of trying, tried that too—All dabbled out—
Bravado
In a vacuum—I—Can—Type—Glosses over—Not
Very fast—

I NEVER STOOPED to charm,
        And for a Southerner,
              Such enormity needs
              No frippery, no accessory.
        Not counting an austere
Naturalistic brooch.
So chic, so chic.

NO WHIMSY in signature
        Details. For whimsy is
              Frigidity too bored
              To be hysterical.
        Who finally would choose
A whimsical Almighty?
So bleak, so bleak.

I NEVER ROSE to brag
        About me, more about me,
              Scarred, cloaked, whatever,
              As if puffs of self-applause,
        The best accessories,
Conquer approaching loss.
So cheap, so cheap.

Another interview with nonsense in it.
My hanging on a hack's every word:
Every obvious banter-bit leads on
To ask-a-doodle-do my qualifications.

A million answers swim the blank that turns
This far, no further. No job offer, vain
The zany can-do grovel . . . Counted on:
Survival of the likable. Big mistake.

Mistake even to shoot back, explain,
Explain how efficiently resilience works,
Produces real tears that count as entertainment

On the way out and pool the nonsense
Shame would like to be remembered
As, remembered as a happy ending.

"THE APPLICANT"

First, are you our sort of a person?
—SYLVIA PLATH

APPLICANT APP

TO THOSE TO WHOM YOU ARE A JOKE
APPLY. APPLY
FAKE CHEER [*repeat*] HA HA GARBAGE
EVERYWHERE YOU LOOK
APPLY. PRY OPEN YOUR LAST RESORT.

CHAT APP

People listen to women who look mass-produced. Blond. Blah
cleaned. Interview these people, please! Who are they? Grill em.
Grill their suicidal kids. The shiny type. Grimly shiny. Fishy.
Fatty? Not self-esteem-y enough. Not to me. In those days,
interviewers padded little questions with the lamest brothel quips.

APPLICANT APP

ARE YOU OUR [*omission*]
LEGAL TO ASK
ARE YOU OUR SORT OF FREE? FREE FROM—
NOT TO, FREE TO—
WHAT [*inaudible*] JOKE WILL YOU APPLY TO?

CHAT APP

Meaning? Pinch me, is that a punch line? Because you need to be
something. Take anything. Pick me. No interview succeeds in a
mink coat, you need to appear needy, not needy, personable. Able
to person? Type. Typecast worker bee. Rush out two, three a day,
the proofs of improving, foolproof. Not to me. O boohoo you.

Awake. Hurt. Hate you
When you lie in bed, hating the day that hurt.

And turning the head,
Hitting it; hurt yet?
Here you hit the pillow with your head,
Thinking, hate to think,

Or will it help to think? You said you hate
Help. Hit the pillow

With your head. Help yet? No, it doesn't help.
Helpless are the hurt
And you should know. Hurt.
Blank it out. Blanket it. Blankety-blank

Before the fear breaks.
Years, your favorite sedative, the rant.

"THE ECONOMIC CRISIS AS IDYLL"

survives in the futile and compensatory determination to be a real adult.
—THEODOR ADORNO

WHEREIN IF wandering out alone
Carry a bit a chaos
Not inherited

Into a vaguely dangerous gamble
Making a killing a win
Before you know it

Windfall profits will be rendered almost
Idyllic or deserving
Or palatable

Practically antiseptic if abstract
Unenviable because
Untraceable a

Stake in silver greens that sting and breezes
Rise as if as if
Anyone edging

Into focus "millions of ambitious"
"Well who are" "they who fail" "who"
"Fail" to resemble

The one who plucks good luck quick off a tree
Carries away a bit a
Fraudulence with luck

Inherits from success a public face
A cosmos to emulate
Try to emulate

Calm seeming calm with apologies to
Nature for unnatural gains
Designed to indulge

    Then that "luxury of pensive sadness"
    Yes only when eating well
    Will you welcome tears

"The lollipops were so superlative"
"Huckleberry" "lime" sugared
Limes and cherry licks

    "An inward perfection of vacancy"
    "Makes my heart go giddyup"
    In arguing calm.

SPEEDING ROUND

AND COUGHING A GALLOP AHEAD OF

UNHAPPINESS

ANYONE CAN LIVE WITH——I CAN

LIVE WITH FATIGUE

WITH DIGNITY

PASSING FOR PHILOSOPHY. "A

BREEZE." GIVEN A CHANCE. "YES INDEED."

SHOUTING—YES, LOUD ENOUGH—AS IF
CONVERSATION,

FRAGRANT ITSELF,

WERE THE ONE PROOF OF EXISTENCE
DESIGNED TO FLATTER EVEN US

WHO WERE LONG AGO DISCARDED—

"HA—" IN THE FOREST, ECHOING
FROM OVER HIS SHOULDER—"HA HA."

"'YOU CAN NEVER'"

I BARK AT HIM, BLOOD A LEAPING,

SPEEDING ROUND, AND
NO EFFORT NEEDED HONESTLY
TO THREATEN HIM

FOR ROUND THE TREES, WALLS—THE HAUGHTY
BARBED PARAPETS—AND GALAXIES
TARGET FAILURE—

"ADVENTURE"—FAILURE—"HA—NICE TRY."

Done in stain-obscuring dark pants pulled on for work
Tossing out the one last second-hand self-help book

Help yourself to hard work is not the half of it
Work hard will never be distinctly natural

Natural is not a camouflage of hard work
Not the plucked waxed dyed in private lines learned

Sensible shoes will open doors the boring doors
Check out the body language of competitors

Jokes at you at your expense required about now
The one about your ow designer shoes ow ow

Supposed to blend in a joke right without the laugh
Resentment is supposed to harden you in life

When laughing at yourself is not a living wage
You can live on for long without a brain-dead brain

From your letter I know you are willing to TAKE
A home, room, board, clothes, an education.
TAKE a punishment, "military punishment,"
For not wearing a tie. And what are you willing

To GIVE? What for a happier home?
What do you propose to contribute to my life?

When you called from jail in Louisiana,
Coherent, agreeable, and nearly sorry,
I told you then to put aside running away,
"Forgetting" to bathe—childish things.

If you come here I shall have to buy a trailer,
And together, we would live in one room.

Inconveniences would be constant, petty,
Personal sacrifices too, and I do not believe
You would comply, finish high school, begin.
You never developed guts enough to slog on.

You liked the laundry job and then you quit.
Did you get your wages, one week's worth,

Or "lose" them, as you did at Gulf Lumber?
I mention wages here because of the money
I sent, and you lost, for your ticket, money
You value as much as the average child of six.

You have not tried living with your father lately.
He might be willing to GIVE all the advantages

Of a nice home, while you live as you wish,
Contributing nothing, a permanent bum.
You are welcome here if you accept discipline.
But if you only leave again, don't come.

Trust, never dominant, recedes. So be it.
So lie in it. You know what I mean.

And certain he was
That his life could be as easily moving down
    Into the crumbling earth as over it,
For whether he was in the earth or of the earth,
    Did it matter, if
        Both were dark and slow?

    Who could be slower than he was, the stones?
He knew the stones admired moonlight and knew
The mice gathered on them, eating snails and
    Singing together
        To the softest moon.

    The weeds were singing
In the night air too, satisfied with a progress
    Few considered perfect or even progress.
Yet everyone considered them progressive.
    True. But have they not
        Been rinsed of malice

    In the vapors of the night? He was certainly
Unmalicious with his feet in the air.
A turtle moment on his back. Entirely turtle.
    And certain he was
        That his life, if now

    Examined, was not
Worth living, but of course, if examined,
    Was it not exposed, and was exposure not a
Form of progress, and progress, however conceived,
    The goal? He had never
        Seen his feet so

Near to dancing as they waved about the moon.
Now the likelihood of another character
Happening by to hear his troubles, turn him over,
    Seemed as small as the
        Weeds; and sure enough,

    Suddenly, he did
What heroes do, confronted by danger, he cried.
    True. And so the weeds stopped singing, mice fled
Far into the crumbling earth, and his comforting
    Assumption that he
        Was moving, moving

    Ahead, faded as he watched his feet and the moon.
And certain he was that, as he waited,
Outsiders in other villages, among the reds
    And cold amber-golds
        And old lush brown leaves

    That darted over
And down, remembered him dearly. Turtle dear.
    And the memory of this, the fantasy
Memory was, moved to certainty as
    Swiftly as the rashness
        Of a young hare.

    Outsiders seemed protected in their morning light,
As if the sun poured a perfect shell on each in turn,
And as the day turned and hardened them,
    They waited for they
        Knew not what alone.

Entirely turtle.
Shell to shell. True. True. If earth is heaven,
      Necessities should be anesthetized.
Have I not been asleep all these years on earth
      As if I were bored
            To tears in heaven?

      And certain he was that his life, herein explained,
Exposed, was, thus, able to move, moving ahead,
However defined. He could hear the weeds,
      Mice too. His feet were
            Dancing on the moon.

One more total loss. And worse
Than a son
Whose value appreciates. From afar.

He will return to military life.
He will will will turn up his
"Purpose." Wayne

Weeps seriously. Didn't
Want to know I didn't want to know him
As crisis.

I can stop him coming home. Hint by hint
If intimacy is not
A story

But a hint.
I can take it. Will will will.
Your dance lessons help. Busy busy hips.

You know how to feed on their defeat
       And find it natural,
            As though the earth exhaled
Its hurricanes and sang,
I'm in the mood for war / simply because you're near me.
       The pity of war you know.

And I was so looking forward to a good war.
       Once more, once more, the trumpets
         Shouting to his buddy
As a rearing horse appraised the trodden gore.

Winning used to be your favorite consolation.
       No? If it be a consolation.
     Be a consolation.
The pity of war you know.

BACK HERE AND rationalize in business terms
Call it a loss call it / a surplus panic

An eye for an eye for an eye for an eye
For enemies are infinite things I think

Back here and internalize as rational
Revenge beefed up / protagonized in public

Eyes take in a beat-up bid for sympathy
A bid overburdened who is last to laugh

Back here and wise up analyze brutalize
All jokes just belligerent / just to survive

OP. "NEW DAWN"

MUST CONTROL STABILITY OPS

WHEN THE NEXT NIGHT APPROACHES AND THE WORLD DIMINISHES

MUST FLY OVER AT A GREAT DISTANCE TO CONTROL

HMMM, as if more lies from on high (on *his* body)
Were (a turbulence) in the mind
(A mind-game heaven, gaming a bodily howl)
Encoded, and more lies (on *his* death)
Were natural, irresistible, and life
In a haze of more lies negotiates—

Is that the word? Just try to negotiate
A haze without clearance (for *his* body)
(For display, for disposal). Life
Clings to little certainties, stories the mind
Lies with awake, until (all hell let loose) death
Calls, and the body cheats or folds? Anyhow,

AT EASE

WHEN THE NEXT NIGHT APPROACHES AND THE WORLD DIMINISHES

MUST LAND BETWEEN PITY AND RIDICULE

ANYHOW,
"Negotiate"
The pity, in theory, death
Provides the body
With the ridicule a mind
Unmade by life

Actually requires—life
Games time, tragedy plus time, however howled
This "stability operation," my . . .

BE SPECIFIC

WHEN THE NEXT NIGHT APPROACHES AND THE WORLD DIMINISHES

WHEN LIES TO LITTLE PEOPLE HAVE A LOGIC ALL THEIR OWN

MY BLUE HOUR slips into something already nauseous,
Red: "Dawn": Jargon: "Operation Iraqi
Freedom" brings on "New Dawn": A thousand new
Dawn stories. Do "Never Wear (off-duty)
A Loaded Gun." Without laughing. Go on.
Though the Army told another story.

YES SIR. And he, turning from a gutted home, heard
The story (Dawn. Off duty. Stars at ease.)
And missed the tree promoted to pearl.
Dust expecting to be next. And heard
Nothing cautionary, helmeted, safe,
When, in a game, the body cheats, the gun cheers.

The birds take up a climax without consequence.
Though the Army told another

DAWN. A different story drives by battered. And he
(Again a brave position on patrol)

Searched the blossoms scattering abruptly.
A mine-field, sincere condolences.

The father bringing for his child a shroud.
Though the Army told

A BETTER new dawn. And he, as hero-class, swerved,
(Rubble?) heard (possible) sniper? Overlit,
(Must be a game, not a game) mocking
Shadow play, from God we came to God we go,
Through stolen cities, herding flocks of dust.
Though the Army

ATTENTION

WHEN THE NEXT NIGHT APPROACHES AND THE WORLD DIMINISHES

MUST LAND IN THE PITY PART SAD

SERGEANT—two of them told her how it went. "Killed
("Next of Kin in Person Told": Yes Sir.) . . . in
House sweep": A story "hazy" officially,
Vague enough for pity, in theory,
In language for the birds, red ones circling
Tragedy plus time, however howled my

AT EASE

WHEN THE NEXT NIGHT APPROACHES AND THE WORLD DIMINISHES

MUST LAND AS INSTRUCTED IN RIDICULE

"WHAT . . . NOW": And he, drawing a gun, played along a
Laugh: Adventure come-of-age laughing:
Ridiculous. Men in summer camouflage
Lock and load, laughing: Quick (their room, Iraq)
Draw: Keep it simple: Shot the other guy.
Though the Army

BUNDLED the story in a story. Accident.
And he started it. "What would you do now":
Shot the other guy. (The game downloaded.
Go on playing sincere, sincere, must
Negotiate, must authenticate a quest.)
Though the Army told

THE COURT they knew not to "wear (off-duty) loaded guns."
And he—they were friends: boys in their one room
Clown around to music with Berettas.
(Sound off: 1, 2: Imaginary
Enemies compete.) Aim fire. And repeat.
Though the Army told another

SCHEHERAZADE, obstructing what still-classified
Approaching dawn? The trial vanishes.
"Behaving badly" "involuntarily" (slap)
Protects enough (the game)? At least enough
For everybody on board peripheral
Reality: A climax without consequence

Imprisoned in an amulet reserved for God?
Though the Army told another story.

BE GENERAL
WHEN THE NEXT NIGHT APPROACHES AND THE WORLD DIMINISHES
MUST FLY OVER AT A GREAT DISTANCE IF OBFUSCATION IS STABILITY

DONE the desert. Done the wind. What other pitiful
Story in a bottle under red sand?

(I miss him but will not send instead of flowers
Cash. Done the flowers. Done the cash.

Lies. Not even . . . never met him. And) he married
Into my family on the other shore.

MUST PROTECT A FORCE STRENGTH
WHEN THE NEXT NIGHT APPROACHES AND THE WORLD DIMINISHES
MUST LAND AS INSTRUCTED AFTER CIRCLING

SAD the other shore, sad for them. How
Someone, willing to die, and so on, goes,
Packaged on a need-to-know basis, my

Army story. Stories protect the mind
With ceremony, certainty, and distance death,
Abstracting waste encoded in negations,
Obvious nonsense, the languorous pace of lies,
Blahs of peace, New Dawn roses: Howlers
Ridicule the body, give it a rest, the body

The game played awhile. The body the mind
Throws a pity bone. Wow. Go on any how.
Dawn pets whatever life death body comes.

"'YOU LIE,' HE CRIED"

FLUNG AFAR ON ANGER—RUNNING,
HIS FEET BLEEDING—
SOMETIMES SEEMS TO MATTER TO HIM.
"YOU LIE," HE CRIED

AT ME! A CRY
UNWORTHY OF HIM. A PITY

ECHOING IN SUCH A LOT OF
LIGHT LEFT TO HIM AS HE RAN ON.

If I am a riddle, I am not a man.
Ain't that the truth. Ain't I a riddle?
If I am a man, I am not a riddle.

If I am a woman, am I a riddle?
Ain't I a woman?
If I am a riddle, I am not a man.

If I am Sophocles, I am not mad.
If I am mad,
If I am a man, I am not a riddle.

If I am tragic, I am proud, middling manly.
If I am proud, am I tragic?
If I am a riddle, I am not a man.

Not a warrior, nor an old man,
Nor an infant's versatile diddle.
If I am a man, I am not a riddle.

If I am a sphinx, my intellect
Unmans you. Ending choice? Chance?
If I am a riddle, I am not a man.
If I am a man, I am not a riddle.

Remember that seriously merry party,
The kid in uniform stumbling over writers
Licking tinsel
Under the orange Christmas tree?

Bless his heart, the kid has "courted" me. Proposed.
I resisted, initially: his youth, his ignorance,
Uncultivated
Life. Unimportant, of course.

I left the last datable, cultivated man
Mid-cigarette, fled home, drank five bottles of beer,
Wrote my own
Atrocious verse and improvised,

Dawn approaching, damn the neighbors, pain on a damp
Viola. Call this culture? Whereas Tommy is
Sincere, kind,
Unusually mentally alert.

Bright eyes. He loves me, and when I write this, his
Deficiencies are nothing, given how eager he is
To learn. And I
Love teaching those I love. I do.

You know the average man says, "English teacher.
Can't talk to you." Tommy said, "English teacher.
Hot diggity!
If I write letters from camp,

Could you correct them, spelling too?" He did.
Wrote regularly for correction, and I held
Nothing back,
Unlike our *tedibly nice* weekends.

He is not as I should have made him, were I God,
But neither am I . . . I know, you know, we all know
Men prefer
Little wives, if the eyes of Texas

Are upon them. If "Little" keeps busy, amused.
So I will leave the university, the fear
Of censure, needing
A job. Marry. I am alive

Again with leaving, teach laughing. Students call:
"My father wants to visit." "Mind if I bring my wife?"
Visitors
In ironed shirts send love. Send love.

ASLANT A HILL—HORIZON-BOUND—
HAPPY HAPPY

"YOU MUST, YOU WANT TO, YOU MEAN YOU
HAVEN'T, HAVE YOU"—

AT EVERY TURN AND ROUND THE TREES

FAILING JUST IN TIME TO BEGIN

AGAIN, BREATHLESS.

BREATHLESS WOULD BE TRADITIONAL.

Anyway, exhausted: getting not a penny
For appearing with
Greengrocers, bull-hearted bullet makers
In zones of virtue with adventurous coal heavers,

Flurries of merchants,

Bear hunters, blowers of jellied gold glass
Form the more perfect . . . performed abundance.
Called then democracy.

What tools! Twirling curios, glittering

On hooks and bragged about, traded. Read right here
Instructions for care,
A conspicuous surplus of care (Who
Washed with a broom an aura of obscurity?)

While readers prefer—
Sorry, darling—sentimental types
To occupations. We did not read this far to read

Hand-tool nostalgias.

We did not read this far to read poorly
Inserted women—the luckless but alluring . . .
Weighted down with dew-

Wet cotton flung in cotton sacks. Again.
Kneels—while a steely, no, fleshy belligerence
Zigzags, advancing
Closer. Fear at work? We did not read

Fine print: multisyllabic assurances (Who
Would not need to be
Assured? fired?), "Sign here" (if actually heard).

Reconciled? Such a comfort, a bargain, before

Dusting off dust bowl
Songs. Hard. Down in the mouth, a brother's tears,
Tired, glowingly alone—nearly as popular
As a father's fear:

Repeated holding hands. Suffering circles:
The credentials of suffering (our, yours, theirs) heard,
The value exchanged:
Sympathy penciled in the margin—"yes."

And meaningless, a mess (underlined), the demands,

Daubs of doggerel
Twirled, glittering (aura of clarity)—
Nothing open at this time but self-reliance.

"Secretary is
Preferable." "I prefer gender-neutral
Administrative assistant." "Office manager."

"I prefer not to"

Leave daughterish temps, disposable sons.
Soft. The quicksilver intimacies of shop talk.
Moonlighting, then, in
Reticent colors, blue—a brown subdued—

Hired, second shift on spec with foreign entities . . .

While readers prefer
Money to sentimental types, money
To emergencies, the moderate anarchy
Poetry absorbs.

O bite-sized fists! O thrills ambiguous
Scatter under capital gains! Funds too immense
To mention . . . hidden

Securities extenuate into
The future reason for optimism when not
Really possible.

Inexhaustible, individual
Wealth . . . contemplated in a comfortable chair . . . and
No need to advise?
Urge? "never touch the principal" when it

Returns like a scapegoat from the grave with interest.

AS IF FEAR, IN TIME, IN NO TIME,
WITHERS INTO

COURAGE, COURAGE

WISDOM—THINK IT RICH? HA AGAIN

HA—ROUND AND ROUND—

O REPARATIVE NARRATIVES—
LOUDER—THE MORE
THE MERRIER.

COIN

Money is always there but the pockets change; it is not in the same pockets after a change, and that is all there is to say about money.
——GERTRUDE STEIN

AND BETWEEN THEM, it passed repeatedly.
"The shine," said one; "the weight," the other.
And when it rolls through their comedy

A token extra in token copper twilight
And floats offshore, a glint on foam
Tossed, waving away, all there is is flight.

"Hey!" And morning light, gold, waves
A million more in the middle of that,
Swimming in profits: nothing sinks. "Hey!"

They waited in the wet sand for returns,
In the changing light, silver afternoons,
And waited after a change, whimpering.

Whereupon the by-now well-tanned coin
Skips the gray amassing surfaces and
Heads, haven to haven, tail too, for joy.

Myself I want . . . . more
And what I assume you shall assume
And why not? *Come closer,* below the grass you love and leaves.

You have yet RESERVES, you old windbag.

Bring them, offer me
Natural GAS . . . . heat you cannot hide
Anymore. *What is known I strip away . . . . I do not ask*
The gas, the vapors
Subterranean . . . DEPOSITED
In rock . . . . Why ask, why

When I can simply DRILL through brittle shale, rearranging
Air among the staggered parallel formations, *whirling*
And whirling . . . . elemental with me,
Down a hundred thousand and a hundred more digressive
Monologues. Brag. Yawp spectacles. ~~*Enough! Enough! Enough!*~~

FRACTURE any atom that resists . . . . pressure from above.
Speak-forth: *Earth! You seem to look for something in my hands.*
They hold open, they enlarge FRACTURES . . . .

And I flush with bright juice the many fissures, with brine, with
Injected sand with
Injected lubricants, and *surging and surging . . . . through me,*
You feel a waste place
Flooded for a final dribble . . . . as I felt, sharing this,
Exceedingly fine.

And I, *a word of reality . . . . ~~I accept Reality and dare not question it,~~*

Accept the hazards
Done and done in my name and to come . . . .

The new normal deliberately bad science to come,
Protective carcinogens to come:
Trade-offs on the move en masse . . . . temporary, probably,
I am aware who they are . . . . as chlorines spill, shimmering
In aquifers . . . . flammables TRADE SECRETS with antifreeze,
Ethyline glycols, and . . . . *Somehow I have been stunned. Stand back!*

And if I forget,
I conduct, I regulate myself,
Investigate my INDUSTRY,

Pleased with my frequently asked questions,
Pleased with COMPLIANCE
Eased . . . . *vapors lighting and shading my face it shall be you.!*
You, your own vista . . . .

And, if equal to yourself, democratic. Very well.

I have ~~having~~ pried through the strata and analyzed to a hair,
The wrong side of history, the earth
Shaving as if envying the moon . . . . I will have been here
On the path heated and funded by . . . .
The parent company an open question in Dubai.

It coaxes me to the vapor and the dusk . . . . motionless
After work, nothing
Do I begrudge, not dogs their sedatives, pigs, manicures,

When more . . . . is waiting for me among
Post-STANDARD transfigur'd PRACTICES.

With lavish attention to inferior materials,
Muted foliage and figures
Out of focus, their certainties, provincial,
Circular, and shared,

Repeated, as what amounts to praise—

But only a fool would fall for praise so repeated,
Numbing, unanimous,
Fall into the wishes of figures like these,
Meaningless equally

To "others" and "the horizon"—or however

Superiors defined. As???? Laughable optimism
About a pecking order . . . ?
As when a vulture, turning to inhale another's kill,
Guesses at a feast

And hovers over, reading it—is it a "real" prospect,

Worth the diving down, the wing work, the old
Analysis of—disappointing
Poisoned gopher scrap? Of aromatic pain, this
Easily digested—

Taste it alone? —this optimism by denial????

Well, denial—travels well as silence, mystified
In greener pastures
In hard-to-articulate Myanmar . . . or Canada.
Give Canada a try

Where pessimism, icier, a given. Some gift.

Satire, like a tourist destination, takes a laughing
Matter only so far—
A wan laugh Saskatchewan will try, nice try—
Roads pickled expertly—

How far will laughing spin out on the sour ice—

Widening circles, no way not wrong naturally, and
Spinning here, equal to
All directions, until I said unto myself, Self,
What else is possible

And go ahead without me. Copied on obliging rock.

IMMATERIAL ARRIVAL

AFTER A JOURNEY—incompetent, incomplete,
And there you have it—

Burning bridges seemed immensely sensible and
Ended, ignited

The open arms, the stroll on air a bridge is—too
Many suspended

Promises—decorations on a melting rail—
And the acrid smell

Over the aftermath, brightened by wind and
Sky—an acquired taste

[And burning like a lack of human interest
An adult inspires]

As the river now impassable—another
Once impossible

System to learn—riffs on rivulets turning rock,
Handsome turbulence,

Foam. And more than competent on foam, completely
Fluent. Affluent.

ACKNOWLEDGMENTS
AND NOTES

The Atlantic: "Perilous Riddle"; reprinted in Lynn Z. Bloom's *The Essay Connection,* 9th edition (Cengage/Houghton Mifflin, 2010); *thebest americanpoetry* online: "The Girl's Will; or, Optimism"; *Hopkins Review:* "Prospect"; *Inertia* online: "'The Applicant'" and "The Fringe Life"; *Kenyon Review:* "Night Heart"; *Poetry:* "Just Now between Positions"; *The Progressive:* "The Pity of War You Know"; *Southwest Review:* "The Boy's Grace; or, Pessimism"; *TriQuarterly*/Northwestern University: "The Buried Life" and "Poems Found in a Dress for Success"; *Yale Review:* "Coin."

"'The Applicant'": Books Sylvia Plath was reading at the time of her death were Erich Fromm's *Escape from Freedom* (1941) and *The Ha Ha* (1961) by Jennifer Dawson. It was Edith Head who advised against a mink coat on a job interview (*How to Dress for Success,* 1967).

"'The Economic Crisis as Idyll'": Thomas Carlyle wrote Ralph Waldo Emerson on turning to poetry for consolation (1867): "We read, at first, Tennyson's *Idyls,* with profound recognition of the finely elaborated execution, and also of the inward perfection of *vacancy* and, to say the truth, with considerable impatience at being treated so very like infants, though the lollipops were so superlative." See the songs "Lollipop" (1958) and, for line 35, "My Boy Lollipop" (1964).

"Op. 'New Dawn'": In memory of Sergeant Matthew R. Gallagher (1988–2011), 6th Squadron, 9th Calvary Regiment, 3rd Brigade Combat Team, 1st Calvary Division, US Army.

"Perilous Riddle": When Sophocles was old, he was charged by his sons with imbecility, dementia, or madness, depending on the account. In his own defense, he read to the jury from his latest manuscript, *Oedipus at Colonus,* which he was still revising. He was acquitted.

Grateful acknowledgment is made to the John Simon Guggenheim Foundation for a fellowship awarded during the composition of the book. The author also thanks Alec Bernstein, Alice Fulton, Richard Howard, James Long, Jerome McGann, and Jacqueline Osherow for critical readings of the manuscript.

CPSIA information can be obtained
at www.ICGtesting.com
Printed in the USA
LVHW110135010920
664665LV00003B/385

9 780807 172636